The Big Bird

By Ramona Rosenberg

Illustrated by Aleksey Ivanov

Target Skill Realism and Fantasy

PEARSON

Scott
Foresman

Jebb, Jill, and Mom wait
for the bus.

"Here is the big bus!" calls Mom.

The bus pulls up.

Jebb and Jill race to the bus.

Mom said, "Look!

The bus has a face!"

"Hop in," calls the driver.

He has a red cap on.

He has a blue shirt on.

"What is that?" said Jill.

"Is it a bird cage?"

"It is a fan!" said the driver.

We take the bus to the zoo.

"It is a nice place!" said Mom.

They see birds of blue, green,

and yellow.

"What is in the big cage, Mom?"
"It is a bird with a green
face, Jill."

"What did you like best?"

asks Mom.

"The big bird in the cage," calls Jill.

"The bus with the face!" calls Jebb.

8